T0129637

THE PRACTICAL STRATEGIES SERIES
IN AUTISM EDUCATION

series editors

FRANCES A. KARNES & KRISTEN R. STEPHENS

Enhancing Communication in Children With Autism Spectrum Disorders

Tammy D. Barry, Ph.D.,
Stephanie H. Bader,
& Theodore S. Tomeny

Routledge
Taylor & Francis Group

NEW YORK AND LONDON

First published 2010 by Prufrock Press Inc.

Published 2021 by Routledge
605 Third Avenue, New York, NY 10017
2 Park Square, Milton Park, Abingdon, Oxon OX14 4RN

Routledge is an imprint of the Taylor & Francis Group, an informa business

ISBN 13: 978-1-59363-409-4 (pbk)

Contents

Series Preface   1

Introduction   3

Autism Spectrum Disorders:
The Trouble With Language and Communication   5

Interventions for Enhancing Communication   10

Techniques to Implement Interventions   27

Facilitated Communication
and Other Alternative Therapies   41

Conclusion   43

Resources   46

References   53

About the Authors   61

The Practical Strategies Series in Autism offers teachers, counselors, administrators, parents, and other interested parties up-to-date information on a variety of issues pertaining to the characteristics, diagnosis, treatment, and education of students with autism spectrum disorders. Each guide addresses a focused topic and is written by an individual with authority on the issue. Several guides have been published. Among the titles are:

- *An Introduction to Children With Autism*
- *Diagnosis and Treatment of Children With Autism Spectrum Disorders*
- *Educational Strategies for Children With Autism Spectrum Disorders*

For a current listing of available guides within the series, please contact Prufrock Press at 800-998-2208 or visit http://www.prufrock.com.

Autism spectrum disorders (ASD) are a cluster of psychological diagnoses also known as Pervasive Developmental Disorders (PDDs; American Psychiatric Association [APA], 2000), which include Autistic Disorder, Asperger's syndrome, and Pervasive Developmental Disorder, Not Otherwise Specified (PDD-NOS), among others. Symptoms of ASD include impairment in three broad areas: (1) quantity and quality of social interactions; (2) language development and qualitative communication skills; and (3) restricted, repetitive, and stereotyped behaviors or circumscribed interests. The focus of this volume is on the second core area of impairment—language and communication—including methods by which to enhance these abilities in children with ASD. Because communication deficits have a large impact on social interactions, research on social skills building, particularly in the context of enhancing communication, also is reviewed. Notably, children with ASD often experience associated problems that are not part of the criteria for their diagnoses but that, nevertheless, complicate the clinical picture. A number of these associated problems (e.g., academic difficulties, deficits in adaptive skills, exhibiting problem behavior such as aggression when frustrated) often are due to or exacerbated by impairments in communication (Volkmar & Lord, 2007). Thus, when working with this population, it is essential to consider interventions that can enhance their communication skills. Likewise, to some extent, the interventions have to consider ways in which to manage associated problems so they do not further impede communication skills building. The overarching focus of this volume is on practical and effective strategies that can be implemented in a school setting.

The goal is to provide the reader with an overview of the many interventions that show empirical promise to enhance both the receptive and expressive communication abilities of children with ASD and allow them to interact more effectively with others. In addition, a broad range of more general behavioral techniques that are used to implement the communication-specific interventions are examined. None of the strategies examined will eliminate all language and/or communication impairments in children with ASD. However, these communication-building and language-enhancing strategies can alleviate these impairments, thus leading to an improved quality of life for children with ASD by: (a) teaching new skills; (b) building on existing skills; (c) fine-tuning emerging skills; (d) providing motivation for the demonstration of mastered but rarely exhibited skills; (e) helping children generalize their skills to new settings and situations; and (f) maintaining acquired skills.

Language Deficits

Language deficits are a core feature of ASD. Children with ASD, particularly those with a diagnosis of autism, demonstrate significant clinical impairment in their language development and the qualitative nature of their communication (APA, 2000). Diagnostically, children with autism typically show delayed language development and lack of compensation with nonverbal behaviors (e.g., gestures). In fact, approximately one in three children diagnosed will never develop functional language (Mesibov, Adams, & Klinger, 1997). For the remaining 60% to 70% of children who do develop functional language (i.e., no quantitative impairment), their language often is deficient in a qualitative manner. That is, these children may develop extensive vocabularies but, nevertheless, have difficulty either understanding or conveying information due to differences in the way in which they process the information when compared to typically developing children.

Children with ASD often exhibit stereotypical, repetitive, and idiosyncratic language that significantly limits its communicative usefulness (Mesibov et al., 1997). For example, echolalia (i.e., meaningless verbatim repetition of previously heard language) is a common symptom (APA, 2000). Some children with ASD engage primarily in immediate echolalia (repeating words or phrases just heard), whereas other children may present with delayed echolalia (repeating something heard up to days earlier, such as a phrase heard on a commercial or television program). Although echolalia can involve long, involved phrases and clearly is language per se, it is not *communicative* language because it is inflexible and is rarely, if ever, applicable to the situation (Mesibov et al., 1997).

Deficits in semantic language also are characteristic of children with ASD, particularly those children who develop only a limited functional vocabulary. That is, they struggle significantly with understanding the meaning of the communication. This impairment is demonstrated through the tendency for young children with ASD to exhibit pronoun reversals—referring to themselves as "you" and others as "I." Later, these same children may overly use proper names in place of pronouns in their language to compensate for their lack of understanding of when to appropriately use specific pronouns (Mesibov et al., 1997). In addition to these difficulties, the language of children with ASD is frequently plagued with idiosyncratic language and neologisms, which are novel words made up by the child (Volden & Lord, 1991). Such language can be easily understood by only those who become familiar with it. For example, children with ASD may call a blanket a "warmy" or ask for their favorite teddy bear by saying, "I want brown hair." Likewise, their speech quality often is abnormal, including problems with speech pitch, rate, or prosody (i.e., rhythm, stress, and intonation; APA, 2000), whereas their speech pronunciation and articulation appear to be intact (Mesibov et al., 1997).

Communication Deficits

Even in the presence of language, there are communication deficits. Children with ASD who have fully functional language often still experience significant difficulties initiating and sustaining conversation with others. Their problems often revolve around deficits with the pragmatic aspects of language (i.e., use of language in social contexts and learning the rules of conversation; Mesibov et al., 1997). Thus, children with ASD may be silent in social situations or, alternatively, they may engage in long, elaborate monologues that are focused on their idiosyncratic interests. Even when the conversation is on a socially acceptable topic, children with ASD may pursue the topic to an odd and dominating level. They may interrupt, engage in inappropriate shifts of conversation, and have difficulty staying on topic (Mesibov et al., 1997). Because of their pragmatic language deficits, children with ASD sometimes provide too much information on the topic at hand. At other times, they may assume the listener knows what they are talking about even when the listener has had no prior knowledge of the topic and, thereby, provide insufficient background information (Mesibov et al., 1997). Both of these presentations impede communication and cause social awkwardness.

Moreover, semantic language deficits often manifest into the use of a limited range of words in conversation, even for those children with ASD who have a fully developed vocabulary (Mesibov et al., 1997). For example, among high-functioning, highly verbal children with ASD, receptive language (i.e., comprehension skills) is typically better developed than expressive language (APA, 2000). Although children with ASD may easily grasp the verbal concept of concrete and tangible objects (e.g., toys, food), they often have problems understanding words with more abstract meanings (e.g., emotions).

Children with ASD who will speak at length about a topic of interest still may have difficulty answering others' questions, again lacking the give-and-take reciprocity that should be natural in communication with others. They often fail to monitor the impact of their conversations or behaviors on other people and may monopolize conversations or walk away while others are interacting with them (Baron-Cohen & Bolton, 1993).

Furthermore, problems with communication among children with ASD are not limited to verbal communication. Nonverbal behaviors, such as eye contact, facial expressions, gestures, and body posturing, also are frequently impacted and further encumber the process of communicating with others.

Clearly, these communication deficits and oddities take a toll on social relationships, including the formation and maintenance of friendships. In fact, even at a very young age, children with ASD demonstrate play skills that are typically below their expected developmental level, often showing impairments in pretend play, symbolic play, and social imitative play, all of which are considered part of the core communication deficits of ASD (Pennington, 2002). Indeed, a hallmark symptom of ASD is an impairment in the development of reciprocal social interaction skills (APA, 2000). Children with ASD engage in significantly fewer social interactions with other children (Koegel, Koegel, Frea, & Fredeen, 2001), and the gap in social interaction and communication skills grows more pronounced over time (Mesibov, 1986).

Additional Issues

With communication problems come other troubles and a need for intervention. When children with ASD are unable to communicate their wants, desires, and needs effectively, other problems arise. As mentioned, social problems among children with ASD often are exacerbated by the problems they experience with communication. Children with ASD also may engage in other characteristic behaviors, such as displaying a tantrum or acting aggressively, because they are unable to successfully navigate their environment with language and other modes of communication (Koegel, 1995; Matson, 2009). Because of their semantic language impairments, children with ASD often experience difficulty perceiving meaning and drawing relationships between ideas and events (Mesibov, Shea, & Schopler, 2004). This deficit may lead to other problematic behaviors—such as not responding to a teacher's requests—not because the child is defiant but, rather, because he or she simply does not understand the request in the first place. The inability to communicate often causes frustration for both the teacher and child, which may further lead to disruptive behavior. Therefore, programs aimed at teaching children with ASD to communicate can be exceedingly beneficial in improving the education of each child and the environment in the classroom, as well as relationships between the child, his or her peers, and adults.

From this overview of deficits in communication—and subsequently social skills—it is clear that children with ASD have a need for clinical interventions that focus on improving their language and social communication. Fortunately, this palpable need can be addressed through innovative clinical and classroom interventions that have garnered empirical support for their ability to enhance communication skills and lead to better outcomes for children with ASD, not only in the areas of language and communication, but also in other meaningful areas.

Interventions for Enhancing Communication

Many intervention techniques have been designed to specifically address the communication deficits that are typical in children with ASD. Children within the autism spectrum are a heterogeneous group—varying from those who are completely nonverbal to those who are high-functioning and have no history of a language delay. Given the dissimilarity in language abilities that is characteristic of children with ASD, it follows that many of the interventions are most appropriate for certain levels of functioning. As such, each of the communication interventions reviewed has been categorized with a level of functioning for the child (i.e., nonverbal children, children with little verbal communication, and high-functioning verbal children with an idiosyncratic communication style). However, it should be noted that these distinctions are not absolute, and many of the interventions can be used across the various levels of functioning.

The Nonverbal Child

Teaching children with little or no verbal communication skills can be extremely difficult and time-consuming.

Nevertheless, it is a task that must be tackled for, as Koegel (2000) argued, the social competence of children with ASD will be judged by their ability to initiate communication with others. Furthermore, "communication skills provide a foundation for social and personal relationships" (Koegel, 2000, p. 388), and the ability, or lack thereof, to communicate influences the ability of a child to self-regulate his thinking patterns and emotional reactions, as well as subsequent behavior. Fortunately, with the most appropriate interventions, significant improvements in communication can be made, even with the nonverbal child.

It is believed that children with ASD have difficulty with communication because they are unable to apply social contexts to language. Noens and van Berckelaer-Onnes (2005) indicated that children with ASD struggle to integrate external stimuli and require more time to process incoming information as it relates to the current situation—almost as if they are seeing the world as a series of individual pictures. In the spirit of using the children's unique cognitive style to build upon strengths and ameliorate weaknesses, the authors suggest capitalizing on their stronger visual skills by using pictures and photographs to communicate, a strategy that has been supported to teach children with ASD a number of different communicative skills.

Bondy and Frost (1994) argued that, beyond differences in the way that communicative information is processed, children with ASD do not receive the same levels of social reinforcement that typically developing children experience when they communicate. Therefore, direct reinforcement may be necessary when first introducing new communication strategies to children with ASD. For example, sign language and the Picture Exchange Communication System (PECS), two methods that are relatively easy to administer in a classroom setting, utilize differential reinforcement (i.e., reinforcing only positive, desired behaviors in order to increase those behaviors while decreasing negative, undesired behaviors) and have garnered empirical support for increasing communication among nonverbal children (Bartman & Freeman, 2003; Bondy & Frost, 1994; Ganz & Simpson,

2004; Liddle, 2001; Schepis et al., 1982; Spencer, Peterson, & Gillam, 2008; Tincani, 2004). In fact, these techniques can be used with low-functioning children and, accordingly, Mirenda (2008) warned that a student's perceived intellectual dysfunction should not limit a teacher's choices of teaching programs, particularly those targeting communication. Both sign language and PECS are meant to teach the most basic of communication skills, but they also provide a foundation on which further skills can be built during later development.

Sign Language

Sign language has been shown to be an effective tool in teaching children with ASD to communicate, even in children as young as 2 years old (Bartman & Freeman, 2003). A number of studies have demonstrated that sign language leads to increased vocalizations (Schepis et al., 1982; Tincani, 2004). Reinforcement, physical and verbal prompts, and manual guidance (i.e., physically forming the child's hand into a sign) have been used to teach children enough signs to make requests, as well as other forms of communication about their experiences (Schepis et al., 1982; Tincani, 2004).

Tincani (2004) discussed teaching children to use the most basic American Sign Language signs for a number of objects, particularly those with reinforcing value, in their everyday life. Because children with ASD respond well to immediate rewards, it is helpful to first teach them signs for objects that are highly desired until they get accustomed to using sign language (Odom et al., 2003; Tincani, 2004). Once these basic signs are established, their signing vocabulary can be expanded to include a broader array of objects and activities.

It is important to use signs that are distinct from one another in hand shape, location of the hand, and movement of the hand in order to avoid confusion among children with ASD (Tincani, 2004). It also may be beneficial to create novel signs that depict a motion that can easily be associated with a particular object (e.g., using two hands as if playing with a Slinky as the sign for that particular toy; Tincani, 2004). The first step—which occurs before the actual training—is to identify objects (e.g., edibles, toys) that the child consistently wants to act as reinforcers (Tincani, 2004). It is preferable to choose a wide variety of reinforcers because, once on hand, new reinforcers can be introduced to replace initial items as the child becomes uninterested in them, thereby avoiding satiation. A hallmark characteristic of ASD is restricted interests (APA, 2000), and so finding an object that the child consistently wants should not be difficult (Bondy & Frost, 1994).

If possible, two adults—one acting as a listener (sitting in front of the child) and one providing prompts (sitting behind the child)—should be involved in teaching signs to children with ASD (Tincani, 2004). First, the child should be presented with an object that is assumed to be a reinforcer and taught the sign for it if he or she reaches for it. If the child is uninterested, the object should be replaced with something new until the child shows interest, because it is critical that initial signs be used for objects that are inherently reinforcing for the child.

Once a salient reinforcer has been identified, the listener will present the object, give the corresponding hand sign, and vocally name the object (Tincani, 2004). If the child does not spontaneously imitate the sign, the prompter should physically guide the child's hand into the proper sign (using a hand-over-hand technique). This ensures a correct signing response for each presentation of the object. After the child performs the sign (with or without guidance), the child should immediately be rewarded with the object. It is important that the listener does *not* give a verbal prompt (e.g., "What do you want?") before presenting the object, because it could distract the child from using the sign or lead to dependence on a verbal prompt (Tincani, 2004). The goal is to teach the child to initiate more communication through signing.

As the child begins to understand the use of signs, the time between presentations of the objects and the vocal and physical models should be increased, which should subsequently increase the likelihood that the child will spontaneously produce a sign for the object without any modeling. Once the child performs the correct sign, it is important for the listener to provide a physical and vocal model and immediately reward the child. Tincani (2004) suggested waiting up to 4 seconds between presentation and modeling; the prompter can still provide guidance as needed on each presentation. It is best to present each object approximately five to seven times until the child becomes satiated with the object, at which time it can be replaced with another rewarding item. Repetition with the same objects across different days should be used until the signs are used spontaneously during nontraining times. At that time, new objects can be introduced during training sessions to teach additional signs and grow the child's communicative vocabulary.

Picture Exchange Communication System

Implicitly learned behaviors, such as direct eye contact, may come naturally to the typically developing child, but be lacking—or at least effortful—in a child with ASD (APA, 2000), which is likely due in part to a lack of experiencing the inherent social reinforcement of those behaviors (Bondy & Frost, 1994). Therefore, fundamental behaviors, such as eye contact and initiating conversations, do not come naturally for children with ASD. Due to this deficit in social initiative among children with ASD, Bondy and Frost (1994) argued that nonverbal children (with or without an ASD) should first be taught to communicate in a way that provides them with a concrete reinforcer. PECS accomplishes this goal by requiring the nonverbal child to exchange a picture of an object in order to obtain the actual object. Thus, rather than learning to label objects (which is vague and requires a social context), the child learns to associate objects with a symbol for that object (i.e., a picture), based on the concrete consequence of receiving the desired object. As in teaching sign language, the first step of PECS is to find a variety of tangible objects to act as reinforcers. It is important for the teacher to observe the child in a natural setting and carefully choose objects that the child finds highly desirable because PECS relies on the reinforcing value of the objects chosen (Bondy & Frost, 1994). Pictures of each reinforcing object also will be needed and should be laminated to increase the longevity of their use.

Bondy and Frost (1994) described six PECS phases (see Figure 1). During Phase 1, the child is taught to exchange pictures of the desired object for the object through physical guidance. The chosen reinforcers should be displayed to determine which one is most preferred. All other objects should be removed. As the child reaches for the remaining object, the teacher should place the picture of the object in the child's hand. Another adult (i.e., trainer) who is seated behind the child should guide the child's hand (with the picture in it) toward the teacher's hand, which should be outstretched to receive the picture. After the child releases the picture to the teacher, he or she should immediately be rewarded with the desired object, accompanied by a phrase such as, "Oh, you want a ___? Here it is!" (Bondy & Frost, 1994). The teacher should avoid mentioning the actual picture exchange but, rather, act as though the child asked for the object. That is, it is important for the picture exchange to mimic natural communication as much as possible. It also is imperative that both the teacher and trainer avoid verbal prompts because the child may become dependent on these prompts. This should be repeated until the child consistently uses the picture in exchange for the reinforcer, and guidance from the trainer should be gradually faded. The child should receive the desired object each time there is a successful exchange; this consistency is key to the success of PECS.

Phase 2 is designed to increase the utility of PECS by increasing both the distance between the child and teacher and the number of people acting as teachers (Bondy & Frost, 1994). During this phase, a board, often using Velcro®, is needed to hold the various pictures. Rather than sitting directly in front of the child, Phase 2 requires that the child, picture board, and teacher be in different locations within the room. Such an arrangement requires the child to travel to the communication board, retrieve the picture, and then find the teacher to make the exchange. The

Phase	Objective	Description
Phase 1	Have the child exchange a picture of a desired object for that object.	The desired object should be presented and, as the child reaches for the object, the teacher should place a picture of the object in the child's hand. The child should then give the picture to the teacher in exchange for the object.
Phase 2	Increase utility of PECS by increasing distance and variety of people acting as teachers.	With the teacher, child, and picture board in three different locations within the room, the child is required to get a picture from the board, travel to the teacher, and give the picture in exchange for the desired object. The person playing the role of teacher should periodically change so that the child learns to use this communication skill with multiple people.
Phase 3	Have the child differentiate between two pictures based on contextual information.	Two pictures should be placed on the board—one that is contextually appropriate and one that is neutral. The child should only be rewarded with the desired object if he or she chooses the appropriate picture.
Phase 4	Promote sentence formation with the communication board.	In order to get the desired object, the child should be required to form a sentence on a sentence strip using an "I want" card (or similar phrase) and pairing it with a picture. The child then can exchange the complete sentence for the desired object.
Phase 5	Have the child respond to verbal prompts.	The teacher should ask the child, "What do you want?" while pointing to the "I want" card. The child should then create a sentence on the communication board using the appropriate cards and complete the exchange.
Phase 6	Expand the child's repertoire of sentences.	New phrase cards such as "I see" or "I have" should be available on the picture board, along with pictures of only moderately desirable objects. The teacher then performs an appropriate prompt (e.g., "What do you see?") while holding up a pictured object. Once the child forms a sentence using the appropriate cards, he or she is rewarded with a small object not related to the object used in the sentence (in order to differentiate between what the child sees and what the child wants).

Figure 1. The six phases of a Picture Exchange Communication System (PECS; Bondy & Frost, 1994).

importance of establishing eye contact to get someone's attention can be emphasized by having the teacher look away as the child approaches with the picture. The trainer should prompt the child to touch the teacher's shoulder or face until eye contact with the teacher is achieved. It is important to continue using questioning phrases (e.g., "Oh, you want a ___?") and to immediately reward the child with the desired object (Bondy & Frost, 1994). Teachers should gradually continue to increase the distance and the number of pictured reinforcers. In addition to requiring more action from the child, Phase 2 focuses on the use of different adults acting as teachers, allowing the exchange technique to generalize to more than one adult.

In Phase 3, the child is taught to differentiate between two pictures based on contextual information (Bondy & Frost, 1994). Based on the child's day-to-day activities, two pictures should be placed on the communication board. One picture should be a desired object that is contextually appropriate for the situation, and one picture should be neutral or not appropriate. The teacher would ask a question, such as, "Which one?" and then point to each of the two pictures. Thus, the child is forced to choose between two pictures. If the child chooses the correct picture, he or she should be rewarded with the object immediately. If the child chooses the neutral picture, a phrase such as, "No, we don't have that one," can be used, accompanied by a gestural prompt (point) toward the correct picture (Bondy & Frost, 1994). If the child struggles with differentiating between pictures, a blank card can be used initially to replace the neutral picture. It is important for the teacher to use a variety of different objects and to vary the location of the target picture on the board so that the child has to search for it. As the child becomes more adept at differentiating among pictures, the teacher can increase the number of neutral pictures to increase the difficulty of the task.

Phase 4 continues to advance the utility of PECS by teaching the child to form sentences (Bondy & Frost, 1994). To embark upon Phase 4, the child should be able to consistently use between 12 and 20 pictures to communicate. It may be helpful to decrease the physical size of the pictures and organize them in a book. Research shows that children using PECS often will vocalize in conjunction with the pictures as they advance through the program (Bondy & Frost, 1994; Tincani, 2004). Therefore, Bondy and Frost (1994) suggested using a card containing the phrase, "I want," paired with a picture. This technique will help to increase the complexity of the child's communicative skills and prevent the use of one-word communication. Again, it should mimic vocal communication as much as possible. The goal of Phase 4 is for the child to pair the "I want" card with a picture on a sentence strip (i.e., a strip of laminated paper on which the two cards can be attached). After the sentence has been formed on the sentence strip, the child should give the strip to the teacher in exchange for the reward. To initially teach this more complex communicative technique, the child should be physically guided to place the "I want" card on the sentence strip followed by the picture. This physical guidance should be gradually faded. It is important to keep the "I want" card in a fixed place on the communication board so that the card can easily be found by the child. As before, the number and variety of pictures should be increased (up to 20 to 50 pictures by the end of Phase 4). Furthermore, teachers can begin to include pictures of objects that are not readily present, such as those that normally may be stored in containers, to increase generalizability.

The previous phases involve spontaneous requests. Phase 5 is designed to have the child respond to the verbal prompt, "What do you want?" (Bondy & Frost, 1994). The teacher should ask the child, "What do you want?" and simultaneously point to the "I want" card that is on the communication board. The child should then select the "I want" card and a picture to complete the sentence (see Figure 2). Gradually, the time between the teacher's question and the teacher's pointing to the "I want" card should be increased until the child completes the sentence without any pointing from the teacher. It is important for teachers to sometimes allow for spontaneous use of the "I want" card so that the child does not become dependent on verbal prompts.

Figure 2. An example of a simple Picture Exchange Communication System board.

Phase 6 is meant to expand the child's repertoire of sentences by including cards with phrases such as "I see" or "I have" (Bondy & Frost, 1994). In order to distinguish from "I want," the teacher should use objects that are only moderately desired by the child. These objects should be displayed on a table with an "I see" card on the communication board, sentence strip, and corresponding pictures nearby. The teacher should hold up an object and ask the child, "What do you see?" and then point to the "I see" card. The child should then complete the sentence using the "I see" card and appropriate picture. The child may need physical guidance early in this phase. Once the child completes the sentence and makes the exchange, the teacher should respond, "Yes, you see a ___," and give the child a small reward that is not related to the object used to make the sentence. In this phase, it is imperative that the reward be different from the object to avoid confusion for the child (i.e., to differentiate between "want" and "see"). It also is necessary to use an object that is not highly desired by the child to avoid unruly behavior due to not receiving the "seen" item.

Bondy and Frost (1994) proposed more complex sentence structures and responses that can be pursued after Phase 6 for children who are more high functioning, including adding adjectives and other verbs, as well as answering yes/no questions. These types of declaratives and questions require social context that can be very difficult for children with ASD.

PECS also can be useful for children who show limited communication but some use of language. With these children, pictures of objects that the child frequently pairs with vocalizations also should be gradually eliminated in order to promote the use of only spoken language for those objects and to promote greater use of their limited vocabulary, as well as possible expansion of their vocabulary. PECS has been shown to be effective in empirical outcome studies, which have documented increased quantity of and improved quality in vocalizations after the implementation of PECS (Ganz & Simpson, 2004; Tincani, 2004). A detailed illustration of the system, including the needed materials, can be found in the PECS Training Manual (Frost & Bondy, 2002).

Choosing PECS Versus Sign Language

Although the consideration of which intervention to implement is a significant one, teachers should be comforted knowing that this often is a decision based on trial and error. It is important to monitor the child's progress; if progress is not being made, the treatment techniques can simply be changed (Spencer et al., 2008). Although the decision often involves trial and error and—oftentimes—false starts, there are ways that families, teachers, and schools can work together to maximize progress and learning. When comparing PECS and sign language, Tincani (2004) found that children responded differently based on their pretreatment abilities. A child with higher preexisting imitative skills may learn sign language more rapidly than a child with poorer imitative skills. Therefore, sign language may be best for children with moderate to high imitative skills (Spencer et al., 2008). The child's motor abilities also should be considered, particularly given that sign language requires fine-tuned manipulations of the hand that may be difficult for some children (Mirenda, 2008; Schepis et al., 1982; Spencer et al., 2008; Tincani, 2004). If the child has poor motor skills and extremely deficient imitative abilities, PECS may be a better fit for him or her, especially if the child enjoys pictures and matching (Spencer et al., 2008; Tincani, 2004).

Children With Limited Verbal Communication

Beyond PECS and Sign Language

Whereas PECS and sign language are ideal for nonverbal children, these strategies also can be used to build upon existing communication skills for verbal children who are limited in their use of language to communicate. However, in an effort to increase their overall use of language and to expand on existing language skills, verbal children also should be exposed to other types of teaching techniques that focus on increasing the quantity and quality of spoken language (Koegel, 2000; Odom et al., 2003). For example, children who use single words or short phrases to communicate should be targeted for expanding to the use of full sentences. In an effort to accomplish this goal, children with ASD who have some vocal communication skills can be taught to use very basic social scripts (i.e., the exact words of what they should say in a very specific social situation; Ganz, Kaylor, Bourgeois, & Hadden, 2008). For example, when conversing with their peers, they may be taught a script to have a brief conversation about what each of them like, such as, "I like dinosaurs. What do you like?" Teachers can direct the communication using index cards with appropriate phrases that act as prompts. Using such techniques, Ganz and colleagues (2008) found a decrease in perseverative talk (i.e., repeating the same word or phrase over and over) and an increase in context appropriate vocalizations.

Verbal Routines and Expansions

Verbal routines (i.e., familiar, predictable activity with verbal interchanges, such as reading a book together) and expansions (e.g., if the child says "doll," the adult says, "The doll is pretty.") can be used to improve the length of verbalizations among children with ASD (Yoder, Spruytenburg, Edwards, & Davies, 1995). Strategies such as these also can be used to help children with limited verbal abilities to use more descriptive language. For example, expansions can help children incorporate more noun-verb combinations, as well as adjectives and adverbs as descriptors (Yoder et al., 1995).

Integration of Verbal and Nonverbal Communication

In addition, children with emergent verbal skills often benefit from strategies helping them to integrate verbal and nonverbal communication, and improvement in one area can be beneficial for the other. Such strategies are based on research that supports the notion that verbal and nonverbal communication is strongly, positively correlated and that nonverbal behaviors—such as joint attention—can impact the verbal trajectories of children with ASD (Anderson et al., 2007). For example, Yoder and McDuffie (2006) reported superior implementation of language therapy following a focus on improved object play and nonverbal communication in young children with ASD with limited verbalizations. They speculated that the children needed to be more fluent in play and nonverbal communicative skills to increase their readiness to uptake verbal language therapy.

High-Functioning Verbal Children With an Idiosyncratic Communication Style

As mentioned earlier, even those children with an ASD who are high functioning and highly verbal typically have problematic communication patterns and oftentimes exhibit an idiosyncratic communication style (Odom et al., 2003). As such, these children also will benefit from strategies that target improved communication.

Answering Questions

Children with ASD who have functional language still frequently have problems understanding or knowing when to use "wh" questions. However, Jahr (2001) demonstrated that, through the use of training sessions focusing on four classes of questions (what, who, where, why) one-by-one, combined with differential reinforcement, improvements can be made. Imitative prompts of the appropriate answers should be provided if the child does not approximate an acceptable response. Again, differential reinforcement involves reinforcing only positive, desired behaviors in order to increase those behaviors, while decreasing negative, undesired behaviors. Thus, only the acceptable responses would be rewarded during training sessions. Through repetition in training and the use of multiple exemplars, Jahr demonstrated improvement to full sentence responses to all four classes of "wh" questions, with a generalization of skills to novel questions, people, and places.

Improving Quality and Understanding of Language, Particularly in a Social Context

Because high-functioning, verbal children with ASD often show the characteristic nonverbal impairments associated with the set of disorders, they are targets for techniques designed to improve their ability to read others' nonverbal communication (Barnhill, Cook, Tebbenkamp, & Myles, 2002), as well as to improve on their own nonverbal skills (e.g., body orientation, making eye contact; Barry et al., 2003). Techniques also have been developed to help children with ASD improve in their ability to understand abstract language and the pragmatics of language (Landa, 2000; Volden, Mulcahy, & Holdgrafer, 1997). Social scripts and social stories (Gray, 2010) can be used to prepare a child with ASD for social exchanges that involve communication. As mentioned earlier, social scripts provide children with the exact language to use in specific social situations (e.g., greeting someone new; Barry et al., 2003). Social stories differ from scripts in that they provide a mix of descriptive, perspective, and directive sentences about a social situation in which the child is likely to engage (Gray, 2010). As children gain in social communication skills, the directive sentences can be faded. Both social scripts and social stories help children with ASD explicitly learn skills that are more implicitly learned by typically developing children.

Due to their pattern of deficits, techniques that improve perspective-taking and reciprocity in communication also are important. For example, vignettes can be presented and children can be asked questions about the thoughts and feelings of different characters in the vignette (Barry et al., 2003). Finally, children with ASD can be given explicit rules about how long or how many times they can talk about their restricted interests during a specific timeframe so that they avoid engaging in monologues. Many of these more advanced social communication techniques are frequently part of social skills groups for children with ASD, as discussed below.

Social Skills Groups

Because pragmatic language impairments and other communication deficits impact the social functioning of children with ASD, including verbal high-functioning children, social skills groups can be used to improve communication skills (Barry et al., 2003; Rose & Anketell, 2009; Ruble, Willis, & Crabtree, 2008). Although discussed within the context of higher functioning individuals, through the use of structuring and setting small discrete goals, social skills groups can be used to improve the communication skills of children with ASD at any level of functioning.

School-based social skills interventions designed to improve the social skills of children with ASD have been shown to effectively increase both initiations and responses during social interactions. Skills can range from initiating and responding to greetings, conversing on a variety of topics, talking during play, giving and accepting compliments, and sharing (e.g., Kamps, Leonard, Vernon, Dugan, & Delquadri, 1992). Social skills groups in clinic settings also can be beneficial (e.g., Barry et al., 2003) and may be an excellent supplement to school-based work, given that many of the interventions in schools are possible for only short time periods.

Regardless of the setting of the social skills group, it is important that it follows a similar, predictable structure. For example, Barry and colleagues (2003) designed a social skills group that regularly included (a) a warm-up activity; (b) a didactic component to teach new skills (typically facilitated by the use of specific scripts); (c) role-play and active practice (engaging in practice with adults, with puppets, or with each other); (d) snack time to promote unstructured practice in a traditional social activity; (e) an assessment period to evaluate skills and to practice with typically developing peers; (f) show and tell; and (g) a report to parents, during which children demonstrated their new skills and homework was assigned.

The content and target skills should change across time as new skills are acquired. For example, over several months, Barry and colleagues (2003) targeted initiating greetings, responding to greetings, initiating conversation, responding in conversation, initiating play, and responding to requests to play. However, the basic structure of the group should follow the same predictable pattern. A key element for the success of social skills interventions on improving pragmatic language deficits and social communication is practice outside of the group, which can be accomplished through homework exercises and other assignments designed to generalize group-learned material to a more natural setting with novel people (Barry et al., 2003). This can be facilitated by providing parents with an overview of what has been taught during the group session, how it was practiced during the session, and how parents could routinely approximate a similar practice at home. Providing parents with an outline of the topics and skills also gives them the opportunity to reinforce target social skills when they naturally occur. Finally, homework can involve a specific activity that allows skills to generalize to new settings. For example, if greeting skills are the target, homework may involve meeting three new people. Again, this should be communicated in writing so that parents and children remember the homework. There also should be something that must be returned to the next group session to show that the homework was completed. For example, the child may return with a list of the names of three new people that he or she met and one piece of information learned about each new person.

Techniques to Implement Interventions

Whereas the previously discussed interventions focus on language and social communication, specifically, it also is important to consider techniques that allow the successful implementation of those interventions. When working with children with ASD to enhance communication, it is not enough to teach new skills and provide multiple opportunities to engage in those skills. It also is imperative that the children are motivated to demonstrate the skills and that other behavioral problems are managed so that they do not impede learning. A broad range of more general behavioral techniques that are used to implement the communication-specific interventions are examined below.

Applied Behavior Analysis

In a seminal article on applied behavior analysis (ABA), Baer, Wolf, and Risley (1968) differentiated this behavioral science from that conducted in laboratory settings by its *application* to real-world settings, including home, clinic, and school settings. According to the authors, the aim of ABA is to address issues in behavior and learning that have an important *social* impact (Baer et al., 1968). ABA procedures have been utilized to assess, manage, and treat children diagnosed with intellectual and developmental disabilities (Saunders, McEntee, & Saunders, 2005). Given the focus on socially important behaviors and consequences, its applicability to children with ASD is apparent and many studies support the use of ABA techniques with them (e.g., Lerman, Vorndran, Addison, & Kuhn, 2004).

ABA procedures focus on influencing change in behavior by a focus on the *consequences* of behaviors. Consequences are classified as either reinforcement or punishment. Reinforcement involves consequences that increase the likelihood of the frequency or duration of a specific behavior in the future, whereas punishment involves consequences that decrease the likelihood of the frequency or duration of a specific behavior in the future (Lerman & Vorndran, 2002; Steege et al., 1990; Vollmer, 2002; Vollmer & Iwata, 1991; Vollmer, Iwata, Zarcone, Smith, & Mazaleski, 1993; Vollmer, Marcus, & Ringdahl, 1995).

Both reinforcement and punishment can be categorized as either positive or negative (see Figure 3). In this context, *positive* involves the application of something, and *negative* involves the removal of something. Thus, in response to a target behavior, positive reinforcement involves the application of something desired and negative reinforcement involves the removal of something undesired. Both types of reinforcement should lead to increases in the frequency or duration of the behavior in the future. Positive reinforcement strategies (i.e., reinforcers, rewards) already have been discussed in the context of interventions throughout this volume. Examples of positive reinforcement include praising a child or assigning him to be "line leader" as a reward for verbally participating in class or giving a child an object after she uses a picture to communicate that she wants the object. These positive reinforcers increase the likelihood that the child will participate in the future. An example of negative reinforcement is giving a child a "free pass" on homework for showing good verbal participation in class or giving a child a break from PECS training after she has completed all trials with

Type of Consequence

	Desired	Undesired
After a response, something is given.	↑ **Positive Reinforcement** Desired consequence follows response. Example: Sam appropriately asks for a cookie and his mom gives him one.	↓ **Positive Punishment** Undesired consequence follows response. Example: Megan gets a note home from school for throwing a tantrum instead of telling the teacher what was wrong.
After a response, something is removed.	↓ **Negative Punishment** Desired state removed after a response. Example: Johnny is not allowed to get the toy his mother planned to purchase after he yelled and said inappropriate words in the store.	↑ **Negative Reinforcement** Discomfort removed after a response. Example: Ashley appropriately asks if she can be excused from the table and her dad allows her to leave.

Figure 3. The relationship between positive and negative reinforcement and positive and negative punishment.

maximum effort. These negative reinforcers also increase the likelihood that she will participate in the future.

In response to a target behavior, positive punishment involves the application of something undesired and negative punishment involves the removal of something desired. Both of these types of punishment should lead to decreases in the frequency or duration of the behavior in the future. Examples of positive punishment include scolding or giving detention in response to an undesirable behavior (such as using aggression rather than words to communicate frustration). This positive punishment should decrease the likelihood that the undesirable behavior will occur again in the future. Negative punishment strategies, such as time-out, having to sit out at recess, or taking away privileges (e.g., computer time), also could be used for inappropriate communication techniques. These strategies should decrease the likelihood that the undesirable behavior will occur again in the future. Negative punishment often is referred to as a *response cost* (i.e., contingent loss of reinforcers that will produce a decrease in the frequency of a behavior; Buckley, Strunck, & Newchok, 2005; Woods, 1982). Response costs are sometimes used in conjunction with a token economy (described below as a means of earning rewards) such that the child loses tokens for inappropriate behavior or for not producing the desired behavior.

Considerations of Reinforcement and Punishment in ABA

In determining reinforcers for ABA, it is imperative to conduct a preference assessment to determine what is actually reinforcing to a child. This course of action is particularly important for children with ASD because some consequences that are naturally reinforcing to typically developing children (e.g., attention or physical touch) may not be reinforcing to children with ASD. Trial-based methods can be used to determine which, if any, possible reinforcers are indeed reinforcing (Fisher et al., 1992; Roane, Vollmer, Ringdahl, & Marcus, 1998). If the child has difficulty making choices, a single-stimulus method should be used. One object should be presented alone to determine how often and how long the child engages with it. If the child can make choices, the paired-stimulus method may be better. Two objects are presented simultaneously and the child's preferred choice is noted. However, if many objects are being tested for preference, this method can be time-consuming because it is necessary to present every possible pair of objects. An advantage, however, is the more accurate distinction between high- and low-preference objects than with the single-stimulus method. Finally, the most time-efficient technique is the multiple-stimuli method. An array of objects are presented, and the child chooses the preferred object. This method can involve replacement (unselected objects are replaced with something new), or it can be used without replacement (the chosen object is removed and the child is forced to choose from a reduced number of objects; Fisher et al., 1992; Roane et al., 1998).

Another consideration in ABA is the schedule of reinforcement (or punishment). It often is difficult, if not impossible, to provide children with a continuous schedule of reinforcement (i.e., reinforcing each time a behavior occurs; Vollmer & Iwata, 1991; Vollmer et al., 1993). Even if feasible, continuous reinforcement is inefficient and difficult to fade. Thus, when the goal is enhancing communication in children with ASD, a continuous schedule is typically not favorable. Other schedules can be much more effective. Consequences can be delivered after either a set number of responses (i.e., fixed-ratio schedule) or after a variable number of responses (i.e., variable-ratio schedule). For example, a child may receive a sticker each time he learns exactly five new signs (fixed-ratio), or he may receive a sticker after learning a number of signs (perhaps a sticker after two, three, five, seven, and eight signs, which averages out to be one sticker for about every five signs; variable-ratio). Consequences also can be delivered for the first response after a set amount of time (i.e., fixed-interval schedule) or the first response after a variable amount of time (i.e., variable-interval schedule). For example, a child may receive 5 minutes of play time after working for 15 minutes on his communication work in class (fixed-interval), or a child may get to go to the restroom if he raises his hand to communicate that he needs to go and at least 30 minutes has passed since the previous time he went to the restroom (variable-interval). There are advantages and disadvantages to each schedule and rate of responding varies, depending on which one is chosen. Therefore, the options should be weighed to ensure that the most appropriate schedule is selected to achieve the specific communication goals for the child with ASD.

There are other important considerations regarding the delivery of reinforcement and punishment (Lerman & Vorndran, 2002; Vollmer, 2002). For example, if an undesirable behavior occurs (e.g., screaming to get something), it should not be rein-

forced. Even if reinforced sporadically, it can be difficult to extinguish such behaviors in the future. It also is recommended that
punishment not be used in isolation but rather that punishment
for an undesirable behavior be coupled with reinforcement for
desirable behaviors. For example, if a child is punished for using
aggressive behavior toward a peer to get something he wants, he
also should be taught more appropriate communication strategies and reinforced for using them. Furthermore, delivering a
punishment at the beginning of a chain of undesirable behaviors
is more effective than waiting until the end because completing
each stage of the chain may prompt its continuation. It also is
important to monitor escape and avoidance attempts, which can
further exacerbate communication problems in the child.

Generalization

Critical to ABA techniques in the enhancement of communication skills, as well as all of the communication strategies
discussed, is the concept of generalization (Stokes, 1992; Stokes
& Baer, 1977), or the child's ability to exhibit newly learned
behaviors beyond the initial conditions set when acquiring the
behaviors. Because children with ASD often have difficulties
generalizing the skills they have learned to new individuals,
settings, places, and materials (Rogers, 2000), it is imperative
to ensure that generalization is specifically programmed into
communication training for children with ASD. Once a skill is
learned in one setting, with a particular teacher and with specific
materials, the skill should be taught in more general settings with
more variation from the initial acquisition phase. Generalization
also is enhanced by using naturally reinforcing and occurring
materials that are likely to occur across settings. Indeed, strategies
should target communication skills that will receive reinforcement in the child's everyday environment. For example, it may
be more important to teach a child to sign or say objects in the
home setting than to sign or say zoo animals, as they often will
have the opportunity to be reinforced for communicating "chair"

or "bed" or "TV" versus infrequently having the opportunity to be reinforced for communicating "giraffe" or "zebra."

Generalization also is improved by training loosely and using sufficient stimuli and prompts so that responding is not restricted to a limited number of conditions (Stokes, 1992; Stokes & Baer, 1977). For example, to teach a child to identify an apple, the same picture of an apple should not be used each time. Otherwise, the child may not generalize his or her communication of the word "apple" to other representations of an apple. Thus, it is better to use multiple pictures of an apple, a toy apple, an actual apple, and varied colors of an apple. In addition to varying stimuli, it is important to provide many examples of the target response. For example, a child's response to the question, "How are you?" should not always be, "I am good." To be an effective communicator, the child will need to be taught a variety of responses to the same question, such as "I am happy," "I am sad," or "I am tired." The child should be reinforced for using the appropriate choice of various responses given the specific set of circumstances. Whereas it is important to train sufficient responses, it is equally important to not do so more than is needed for generalization (it is neither necessary nor preferable to attempt to train across all settings). Finally, general case programming encapsulates many of these principles by using varied stimuli, teachers, settings, and materials (Stokes, 1992; Stokes & Baer, 1977). For example, when teaching greeting skills, the child can practice greetings with puppets or dolls, practice greetings in role-plays, greet teachers, greet peers, and then greet people he or she does not know.

Discrete Trial Training

Discrete trial training (DTT) is a specific ABA method used to maximize learning that has been widely applied to children with ASD (Goldstein, 2002; Skokut, Robinson, Openden, & Jimerson, 2008), including for the purposes of increasing communication skills. DTT involves breaking complex skills into small, discrete steps. Each step is intensely focused upon, with repetition and positive reinforcement procedures being key, until the skill is mastered. Although prompts are used, they are faded as soon as possible (Goldstein, 2002; Skokut et al., 2008). ABA therapy sessions use repeated trials, each of which has a distinct (i.e., *discrete*) beginning, middle, and end. In DTT, a child's response to a small part of a skill is immediately reinforced (or not reinforced), depending on the execution of the skill.

For example, if DTT were being used to implement sign language, an entire session may focus on teaching a child to sign for a cookie. Following the procedures described for sign language earlier (Tincani, 2004), the discrete trials would consist of the child being presented with the cookie and being prompted, "What do you want?" The child then has to attempt to make the sign for "cookie." If the child attempts to sign the word, the adult should model the correct way to sign it and then provide the child with the cookie. The child should continue on this specific step until it is mastered without prompting. Once the sign is mastered and part of the child's communicative repertoire, the child should be required to sign the word "cookie" correctly in order to receive a cookie (i.e., use his or her known communication).

A prerequisite skill for DTT is the ability to sit and attend at a workstation. In fact, simply being able to follow the directive, "come sit," often is one of the first goals of DTT. Once a child can sit at a workstation and attend to directions without showing behavioral problems (e.g., tantrums, aggression), he or she is ready to be introduced to more complex tasks, including social and communicative tasks (Goldstein, 2002; Skokut et al., 2008). DTT is designed to increase the likelihood that the child will act in desirable ways by utilizing the reinforcement techniques previously described (Goldstein, 2002; Skokut et al., 2008). The child is presented with the reinforcer immediately following the correct response. Once the response has been mastered, the reinforcement is then faded and the response is generalized to the natural setting. This is accomplished by decreasing the frequency of reinforcement or changing the schedule of reinforcement and employing the generalization procedures previously described.

Functional Assessment of Behavior

When considering which new behaviors to teach, which behaviors to extinguish or replace, and which communication skills to teach a child, it is essential to consider not only the behaviors that the child currently exhibits but also the function of those behaviors. A functional assessment of behavior provides a detailed description of behavior, the context in which it occurs (antecedents), and the consequences it yields, to not only better understand the behavior but also those factors possibly influencing it (Carr, Yarbrough, & Langdon, 1997; Dunlap, Kern-Dunlap, Clarke, & Robbins, 1991; Iwata, Dorsey, Slifer, Bauman, & Richman, 1994; Northup et al., 1991). A functional behavior analysis begins as an assessment, but includes intervention, which is accomplished by altering behavioral antecedents and consequences.

A functional behavior assessment begins with careful observation and description of the behavior (B) as well as its antecedents (A) and consequences (C)—or ABCs (Carr et al., 1997; Dunlap et al., 1991; Iwata et al., 1994; Northup et al., 1991). To best understand the function of a behavior, it should be observed and described across numerous environments and occasions. Data from these observations should be analyzed to ascertain trends in the occurrences of behavior, as well as to determine the stimuli that may trigger it and the function(s) that it may serve. Hypotheses regarding the functions of the behaviors should be formed and systematically evaluated by altering antecedents and consequences.

Functional Communication Training

Functional Communication Training (FCT) is a method used to replace maladaptive and inappropriate communication behaviors with more appropriate ones (Carr & Durand, 1985; Carr, Newsom, & Binkoff, 1980; Kahng, Iwata, DeLeon, & Worsdell, 1997). FCT involves identifying (through a functional behavioral assessment) the function or purpose of the child's inappropriate behavior. That is, what is the child trying to communicate? Next, FCT involves teaching the child a more appropriate communication skill to reach the same goal (Carr & Durand, 1985). For example, a child who hits his mother when he wants something to eat can be taught to sign or point to a picture of what food he would like to eat, using PECS instead. To be effective, this new form of communication should be within the child's skills repertoire (e.g., pictures, signs, gestures, speech) or easily taught to the child, and it should be clearly noticed and responded to when the child uses it (Carr & Durand, 1985).

Once the communication behavior has been selected, FCT involves ignoring the maladaptive behavior and prompting and acknowledging the use of the new communication behavior (Kahng et al., 1997). Natural opportunities to encourage and acknowledge the replacement behavior should be heeded to guarantee that all of the child's new communicative requests are honored during intervention especially early. Two cautionary notes are in order with FCT. First, the child may experience an extinction burst, which involves an initial increase in a maladaptive behavior before it decreases. At first, the child may think he or she simply has to do more of the maladaptive behavior to get to the same end. Second, the new communication behavior has to be more effective in serving the original function of the maladaptive "communication" in some way (Carr et al., 1980). This often is the case, given that the child is using a more direct form of true communication about her wants and needs rather than communicating in a maladaptive fashion that she simply wants or needs something. For example, a child who hits when hungry may get fed but is more likely to get his food of choice by using PECS to communicate what he wants to eat.

Techniques From TEACCH (Treatment and Education of Autistic and related Communication-handicapped Children)

The TEACCH program focuses on the idea of a culture of autism (i.e., that children with ASD have a different world view than typically developing children; Mesibov et al., 2004). One hallmark of the culture of autism is communication problems, particularly the social use of language. This culture of autism is manifested in various other ways, including a strength in visual information (relative to language), an attention to details but difficulty understanding the meaning of them, and difficulty with combining and/or organizing ideas. Other issues specific to the culture of autism include problems with time concepts, sensory preferences and avoidances, and an attachment to routines and specific interests (Mesibov et al., 2004).

TEACCH is designed to develop skills for the child with ASD by understanding and working within the culture of autism. The physical environment is individually designed to minimize distractions and to use visual cues (e.g., prompts and icons) and supports (e.g., picture schedules) that make daily activities and individual tasks recognizable and predictable (Mesibov et al., 2004). TEACCH programs are used to instruct in and build upon a variety of skills through task completion and also are designed to increase meaningful, spontaneous language (Mesibov et al., 2004). So, for example, in a TEACCH program, a child with ASD may have a picture schedule that shows he will work through three baskets of tasks and then earn play time, and then work through three more baskets of tasks to earn a snack. Each basket would have a picture of the task to be completed and the task would be in the basket. If communication is the goal, the tasks could be oriented toward building communication skills that would vary depending on the verbal functioning of the child. For example, the child could be asked to point to objects as they are named (receptive communication), say the name of objects (expressive communication), complete a puzzle for which a piece is missing and verbally request the missing piece, or answer a series of "wh" questions on a card. Communication can even be demanded for the play or snack break. For example, the child may have to verbally indicate his choice for a toy or a snack from a list of choices. For nonverbal children, this can be accomplished through a picture choice board.

Token Economy System

A token economy system involves rewarding a child with tokens earned for demonstrating a specific behavior that can be used to "buy" an object or activity that he or she desires (Matson & Boisjoli, 2009). A token economy system can be used to increase any form of desired behavior, including communication skills. It is a more natural form of reinforcement than either continuous reinforcement or the reinforcement schedules previously discussed (Matson & Boisjoli, 2009). Token economies can range from brief and simple to complex systems (Matson & Boisjoli, 2009). Various tokens can be used, such as stickers, check marks, or poker chips. The tokens can be used to either gain a reward immediately or in the future. For example, a child could earn a token after answering five questions correctly on a token board. Once the child has earned the requisite number of tokens, he or she can obtain an immediate reinforcer, such as a piece of cookie. At the beginning of each session, the child should be reminded that five questions must be answered correctly to get the piece of cookie, while the teacher is pointing to the corresponding parts on the token board. Each time that the child answers a question correctly, the child gets to add another token to the board. When the board has all five tokens, the child gets the piece of cookie. The token economy is then reset. This system allows for the fading of reinforcement by gradually increasing the number of tokens required.

A token economy system should clearly provide a visual representation of how much the child has accomplished and how much more he or she needs to accomplish before reinforcement is delivered. Token economies should be individualized for each child; address specific, targeted behaviors; and clearly communicate the expectations and rules to that particular child in a manner he or she can understand. It is best to allow the child to choose the reinforcer, within reason, because it mimics real-world reinforcement more closely, develops his or her decision-making skills, and is typically more reinforcing (Cannella, O'Reilly, &

Lancioni, 2005). Verbal praise should always be paired with the presentation of both the tokens and the reinforcer. Praise for communication skills could include, for example, "great job using your words," or "great job signing what you wanted." This will remind the child why he or she is receiving the token and help to establish social praise as a reinforcer (Cotler, Applegate, King, & Kristal, 1972). Finally, response costs can be built into a token economy, whereby a child loses tokens toward privileges for demonstrating inappropriate behavior (e.g., aggressing instead of using words to communicate frustration) or for not demonstrating desired behaviors at key points (e.g., refusing to sign during a sign language training session).

Milieu Training

In milieu training for communication, teaching episodes are naturally woven into routine activities in a child's everyday environment, such as dinner and bath time (Goldstein, 2002). Teaching begins when the child shows interest in activities or materials, such as picking up a toy or object. Through the use of prompts—including modeling, asking questions, or making requests—the child is taught to use his or her language skills to communicate about the environment. Any communicative responses are rewarded with natural consequences that would occur as a result of communication (e.g., a child that requests a snack is given a snack). Sometimes the environment is manipulated in order to provide specific opportunities for natural teaching—or incidental learning.

Typical Peer Buddy System

A typical peer buddy system can be used to allow opportunities for modeling of appropriate social communicative skills and increased peer interaction. First, the typically developing peers must be educated and trained about ASD, including ways to engage a child with ASD in social exchanges (Goldstein,

Kaczmarek, Pennington, & Shafer, 1992; Laushey & Heflin, 2000). Books and other resources are available for this training, such as the *Sixth Sense* program by Carol Gray (2002). Broadly, the peer buddies are taught (through the use of scripts) to stay, play, and talk with their buddy (Laushey & Heflin, 2000). Specifically, they are taught skills, such as turn-taking, establishing mutual attention, and commenting/describing, that can be modeled to the child with an ASD.

To maximize success, typically developing peers must master these strategies (through role-plays with and verbal feedback from adults) before using these facilitative strategies with classmates with ASD (Bass & Mulick, 2007). Teachers should watch the buddy interchanges so that prompts can be used to remind the typically developing peer buddy to use specific techniques. Likewise, praise and reinforcement can be given when the techniques are used (Bass & Mulick, 2007).

The peer buddy system is particularly helpful in increasing the quantity of responses by children with ASD (Rogers, 2000). However, a combination of a social skills intervention directly with the child with ASD and a peer buddy system can be successful in improving both initiation and responses by the child with ASD (Barry et al., 2003). Improvements in both quantity and quality of these social interchanges can be seen when using a peer buddy system.

Facilitated Communication and Other Alternative Therapies

A volume on enhancing the communication of children with ASD would be remiss if it did not address facilitated communication and other alternative therapies. Facilitated communication came to the United States in the early 1990s, introduced by Biklen (1990), primarily to work with individuals with ASD and comorbid severe intellectual disabilities. Claims have been made that roughly 9 out of 10 individuals with ASD thought to be nonverbal are able to communicate via facilitated communication, which involves communicating on a computer or some variation of a keyboard or augmentative communication device (with the hand or arm supported by a facilitator; Mesibov et al., 1997). Although there are anecdotal success stories, there is much controversy surrounding the use of facilitated communication with children with ASD. At the very least, it can be determined that there is currently a lack of empirical support regarding its efficacy as an intervention tool. A review of the literature shows that hundreds of clients who communicate via facilitated communication are unable to do so without a facilitator (Mesibov et al., 1997), suggesting that it may be the facilitator who (even unknowingly) may be doing the communication (Finn, Bothe, & Bramlett, 2005).

A lack of empirical support describes many other alternative therapies that often are touted on the Internet and in the popular media, such as special diets, dolphin therapy, hippotherapy (i.e., using unique movements of a horse to achieve health goals), Hyperbaric Oxygen Treatments, and color or light therapy, among others (Gasalberti, 2006; Granpeesheh et al., 2009). Along with a lack of evidence of their efficacy, many of these techniques are extremely expensive and possibly dangerous (Finn et al., 2005; Granpeesheh et al., 2009). It is important that parents, teachers, and caregivers consider the scientific merit of alternative therapies (Finn et al., 2005), particularly given their vulnerabilities in wanting to do all that they can to help their child with special needs (Mesibov et al., 1997).

Conclusion

This volume has offered many strategies available to enhance the communication skills of children with ASD. In fact, there are so many options that it may appear that any child could work his or her way up to fully functional, socially appropriate language. A word of warning is in order, however. Whereas there are some anecdotal cases where children improved dramatically and to the point that impairment was no longer apparent, these cases are atypical and not representative of the usual course and prognosis of ASD. Thus, teachers and other caregivers are cautioned to have realistic expectations about communication improvement in children with ASD. They should expect that improvements will take a great deal of work, come in small doses, and appear gradually over time.

Identifying the Most Effective Strategies

Which strategies are the most effective? Through a review of the current literature, Odom and colleagues (2003) grouped a number of different communication-enhancing strategies based on their perceived effectiveness. The two communication strategies that were found to be well established in the empirical literature are techniques involving differential reinforcement for appropriate responding and adult prompting (e.g., modeling, reminding, social scripts, social stories; Ganz et al., 2008) to initiate appropriate communication. Normally, the prompting is gradually faded as the child progresses. Odom et al. (2003) grouped peer-mediated (e.g., typically developing peer buddy system), visually mediated (e.g., PECS, sign language), self-monitoring, and school/family-initiated techniques (e.g., social skills groups) into effective and developing strategies. The authors explained that these techniques are shown to be effective, yet they are still in their early phases of development and empirical inquiry. Other strategies listed by Odom et al. (2003) that are probably effective, but lack substantial supporting evidence, include positive behavior support (i.e., targeting secondary behavioral problems that often accompany ASD so that communication can then be addressed), modeling using videotapes, and child preference, where the child chooses the type of learning.

Selecting the Best Strategy

With so many effective choices, how does one select the best strategy for a child? When choosing a treatment plan, teachers should consider the characteristics of the child, the pretreatment communication patterns, the preferences of the family, and the available resources (Spencer et al., 2008). A child's improvements, or lack thereof, often are due to the matching of the child's pre-existing skills or deficits with the chosen communicative strategy (Ganz & Simpson, 2004; Tincani, 2004). Therefore, the consideration of the child's current functioning is critical. If a strategy is too simple for the child and targets skills that are already in place, no improvements will be made. If the strategy is too difficult for the child's current functioning, it may cause significant frustration, again impeding improvement. In either of these cases, new strategies that are a better fit for the child should be considered.

Notably, many, if not all, of these strategies require significant collaboration between teachers and family members (e.g., Liddle, 2001; Spencer et al., 2008). Therefore, support and involvement from families is essential. Regardless of the communicative techniques used, the child will need to use the techniques in settings outside of school to make it a regular part of his or her life. Thus, if the family prefers one technique over the other, their requests should be considered. However, if the family's preference could be counterproductive to the child's learning, it is essential that, in an effort to reach a compromise, teachers educate the parents about the different strategies and explain why one may be more beneficial than another for their child.

If the family does not have any strong preferences and the child's characteristics do not definitively indicate a specific technique, teachers should consider what the school may have to offer (e.g., qualifications of interventionists, resources within the classroom; Spencer et al., 2008). The last and most important step is to monitor the child's progress. It is difficult to know with certainty which technique is best for the child until it is actually implemented. Hence, if a child is not responding or improving, the program may need to be adjusted to his or her needs. With ongoing monitoring for continuous improvement, a combination of these communication-building and language-enhancing strategies can lead to measurable progress in the communication skills, and quality of life, of the child with an ASD.

Resources

American Psychological Association
http://www.apa.org/topics/autism/index.aspx
The mission of the American Psychological Association is to advance the creation and application of knowledge that improves individuals' lives and benefits society at large. A large part of this mission involves the communication of this knowledge. At the autism topic site, individuals can access information about ASD and the latest news on ASD, get links to books and articles on ASD, and find ways to get help (including locating a psychologist).

American Speech-Language-Hearing Association
http://www.asha.org/public/speech/disorders/Autism.htm
The overall mission of the American Speech-Language-Hearing Association is to make effective communication accessible and achievable for all individuals. The association promotes effective communication as a human right. At the autism topic site, answers to several important questions about ASD are provided,

including what autism is, how it is diagnosed, and how it is treated.

Autism Research Institute

http://www.autism.com

This is the site of the Autism Research Institute, which is devoted to conducting and disseminating research on risk factors, assessment, and treatment for ASD. The institute provides resources for parents, professionals, and researchers.

Autism Society

http://www.autism-society.org

Autism Society aims to increase public awareness about ASD, advocates for individuals with ASD, and provides details about the latest research information on ASD. The site provides links to the society's grassroots chapters and national partners in order to build a broad autism community.

Handspeak

http://www.handspeak.com

Handspeak is a leading online sign language site, offering an American Sign Language dictionary, grammar, fingerspelling and sign lessons, and storytelling.

National Institute of Mental Health

http://www.nimh.nih.gov/health/publications/autism/complete-index.shtml

The National Institute of Mental Health is an institute in the National Institutes of Health. Its mission is to acquire knowledge that prevents and cures mental illnesses. At the autism topic site, readers can find information on causes, diagnosis, and treatment of ASD, including information specific to adults with ASD.

National Institute on Deafness and Other Communication Disorders

http://www.nidcd.nih.gov/health/voice/autism.htm

The National Institute on Deafness and Other Communication Disorders is an institute in the National Institutes of Health. Its mission is to acquire knowledge that improves health in the areas of hearing, balance, smell, taste, voice, speech, and language. At the autism topic site, readers can find information on how ASD affects communication and how speech and language problems are treated.

Picture Exchange Communication System (PECS)

http://www.pecs-usa.com

Pyramid Educational Consultants, Inc. is a service offering consulting and products for individuals with an ASD and related disorders. The organization also is the exclusive source for training and consultation in PECS, which can be accessed at this site.

The Gray Center for Social Learning and Understanding

http://www.thegraycenter.org

This is the official website for Carol Gray and social stories. The site provides information on what a social story is and how to write one, among other resources.

University of Michigan Autism & Communication Disorders Center

http://www.umaccweb.com

The mission of the University of Michigan Autism & Communication Disorders Center is to improve the lives of individuals with an ASD, as well as the lives of their families. It aims to accomplish this mission through education, research, and clinical services. This website details its mission, research, education/training, and clinical services. It also provides information on diagnostic tools and other resources.

University of North Carolina TEACCH Autism Program
http://www.teacch.com
TEACCH is part of the University of North Carolina School of Medicine. TEACCH provides clinical services for individuals with ASD, conducts training programs for professionals working with individuals with ASD, and performs educational, biomedical, and psychological research aimed at improving the lives of those with ASD. This website details the program's mission, regional centers, programs and services, and trainings. It also provides general information on ASD and links to publications and research.

Books

Ashcroft, W., Argiro, S., & Keohane, J. (2010). *Success strategies for teaching kids with autism*. Waco, TX: Prufrock Press.
The authors provide strategies for incorporating established communication and educational methods into a classroom setting, as well as review the rationale and utility of those methods.

Bogdashina, O. (2005). *Communication issues in autism and Asperger syndrome: Do we speak the same language?*. London, England: Jessica Kingsley.
This theoretically-based book presents models of language acquisition and reviews theories of sensory perception and social deficits of children with ASD. The authors discuss the interplay between these factors. Strategies for enhancing communication based on these theories also are presented.

Bondy, A., & Frost, L. (2002). *A picture's worth: PECS and other visual communication strategies in autism (topics in autism)*. Bethesda, MD: Woodbine House.
This book explores the relationship between language deficits and maladaptive behavior and provides an alternative form of communication, PECS, to help alleviate the frustration that non-verbal children often experience.

Charman, T., & Stone, W. (Eds.). (2006). *Social and communication development in autism spectrum disorders: Early identification, diagnosis, and intervention.* New York, NY: Guilford Press.
This volume provides an in-depth review of screenings, assessment, and diagnosis of ASD as well as evidence-based interventions, including those for language development and augmentative or alternative communication systems.

Farrell, M. (2006). *The effective teacher's guide to autism and communication difficulties: Practical strategies.* New York, NY: Routledge.
This guide sections the overall category of communication difficulties into its components, such as difficulties with speech, grammar, meaning, comprehension, use, and interaction in order to help teachers target these deficits.

Freeman, S., & Dake, L. (1997). *Teach me language: A language manual for children with autism, Asperger's syndrome and related developmental disorders.* Langley, B.C., Canada: SKF Books.
This extensive manual covers how to teach language to children with ASD. It includes strategies, examples, rationales, and explanations for drills and tasks in the areas of social language, general knowledge, grammar, syntax, and advanced language.

Grandin, T. (2006). *Thinking in pictures, expanded edition: My life with autism.* New York, NY: Vintage Books.
Written from the perspective of someone who has autism, this book sheds light on her experience with her diagnosis, visual thought, sensory problems, and lack of innate emotional empathy, as well as how she developed her own specific talents through her relationship with animals and understanding of animal thought.

Gray, C. (2010). *The new social story book* (10th ed.). Arlington, TX: Future Horizons.

This book provides detailed instructions on how to create an effective social story for a child at any communication level. In addition, more than 150 social stories that target common areas of concern, such as introducing oneself, are supplied.

Gray, C. (2002). *The sixth sense II.* Arlington, TX: Future Horizons.
The author discusses activities and lesson plans for educating general education students to be sensitive to the needs of children with ASD, as well as how to interact with these children appropriately.

Hodgdon, L. A. (2000). *Visual strategies for improving communication: Practical supports for school and home.* Troy, MI: QuirkRoberts Publishing.
This book provides detailed explanations and examples on how to use visuals to help improve the child with ASD's communication skills in all settings. These visuals can help organize the environment, aid instruction delivery, provide order to the daily routine, and ease transitions.

Koegel, R. L., & Koegel, L. K. (1995). *Teaching children with autism: Strategies for initiating positive interactions and improving learning opportunities.* Baltimore, MD: Brookes.
The authors instruct parents, educators, and professionals in how to identify teachable moments in order to improve communication and overall interactions with the child with ASD. The book also focuses on the broader context of the family, their stress, and the collaborative relationship between parents and professionals.

Luiselli, J. K., Russo, D. C., Christian, W. P., & Wilczynski, S. M. (Eds.). (2008). *Effective practices for children with autism: Educational and behavioral support interventions that work.* New York, NY: Oxford University Press.
This book emphasizes evidence-based practices, program practice guidelines, behavior interventions and support, and proce-

dures for increasing skills within the overall context of educating children with ASD, which includes increasing the child's communication abilities.

McClannahan, L. E., & Krantz, P. J. (2005). *Teaching conversation to children with autism: Scripts and script fading.* Bethesda, MD: Woodbine House.

In this volume, the authors discuss the use of conversation scripts for children at all language ability levels, including how to write one, implement it, and then fade the usage of it. The book also provides examples and data sheets to track the child's progress.

Matson, J. L. (Ed.). (2009). *Applied behavior analysis for children with autism spectrum disorders.* New York, NY: Springer.

The author provides an overview of ABA and its application to addressing issues such as communication deficits, social skills, and noncompliance. Important issues, such as generalization and maintenance of the learned behaviors, also are discussed.

Mesibov, G. B., Shea, V., & Schopler, E. (2004). *The TEACCH approach to autism spectrum disorders.* New York, NY: Springer.

This volume presents the TEACCH approach to educating children with ASD and its applicability and utility to increasing language and social skills, decreasing disruptive behaviors, and the utility of the program for parents in the home environment.

Potter, C., & Whittaker, C. (2001). *Enabling communication in children with autism.* London, England: Jessica Kingsley.

The authors take the reader through the steps of increasing a child's communication starting with a minimal speech approach and developing to spontaneous communication. The book includes descriptions on how to create a communication-rich environment, facilitate interactions, and develop and manage a classroom to promote communication skills.

References

American Psychiatric Association. (2000). *Diagnostic and statistical manual of mental disorders* (4th ed., Text rev.). Washington, DC: Author.

Anderson, D. K., Lord, C., Risi, S., DiLavore, P. S., Shulman, C., Thurm, A., . . . Pickles, A. (2007). Patterns of growth in verbal abilities among children with autism spectrum disorder. *Journal of Consulting and Clinical Psychology, 75,* 594–604.

Baer, D. M., Wolf, M. M., & Risley, T. R. (1968). Some current dimensions of applied behavior analysis. *Journal of Applied Behavior Analysis, 1,* 91–97.

Barnhill, G. P., Cook, K. T., Tebbenkamp, K., & Myles, B. S. (2002). The effectiveness of social skills intervention targeting nonverbal communication for adolescents with Asperger syndrome and related pervasive developmental delays. *Focus on Autism and Other Developmental Disabilities, 17,* 112–118.

Baron-Cohen, S., & Bolton, P. (1993). *Autism: The facts.* New York, NY: Oxford University Press.

Barry, T. D., Klinger, L. G., Lee, J. M., Palardy, N., Gilmore, T., & Bodin, S. D. (2003). Examining the effectiveness of an outpatient clinic-based social skills group for high-functioning children with autism. *Journal of Autism and Developmental Disorders, 33,* 685–701.

Bartman, S., & Freeman, N. (2003). Teaching language to a two-year-old with autism. *Journal on Developmental Disabilities, 10,* 50–53.

Bass, J. D., & Mulick, J. A. (2007). Social play skill enhancement of children with autism using peers and siblings as therapists. *Psychology in the Schools, 44,* 727–735.

Biklen, D. (1990). Communication unbound: Autism and praxis. *Harvard Educational Review, 60,* 291–314.

Bondy, A. S., & Frost, L. A. (1994). The picture exchange communication system. *Focus on Autistic Behaviors, 9,* 1–19.

Buckley, S. D., Strunck, P. G., & Newchok, D. K. (2005). A comparison of two multicomponent procedures to increase food consumption. *Behavioral Interventions, 20,* 139–146.

Cannella, H. I., O'Reilly, M. F., & Lancioni, G. E. (2005). Choice and preference assessment research with people with severe to profound developmental disabilities: A review of the literature. *Research in Developmental Disabilities, 26,* 1–15.

Carr, E. G., & Durand, V. M. (1985). Reducing behavior problems through functional communication training. *Journal of Applied Behavior Analysis, 18,* 111–126.

Carr, E. G., Newsom, C. D., & Binkoff, J. A. (1980). Escape as a factor in the aggressive behavior of two retarded children. *Journal of Applied Behavior Analysis, 13,* 101–117.

Carr, E. G., Yarbrough, S. C., & Langdon, N. A. (1997). Effects of idiosyncratic stimulus variables on functional analysis outcomes. *Journal of Applied Behavior Analysis, 30,* 673–686.

Cotler, S. B., Applegate, G., King, L. W., & Kristal, S. (1972). Establishing a token economy program in a state hospital classroom: A lesson in training student and teacher. *Behavior Therapy, 3,* 209–222.

Dunlap, G., Kern-Dunlap, L., Clarke, S., & Robbins, F. R. (1991). Functional assessment, curricular revision, and severe behavior problems. *Journal of Applied Behavior Analysis, 24,* 387–397.

Finn, P., Bothe, A. K., & Bramlett, R. E. (2005). Science and pseudoscience in communication disorders: Criteria and applications. *American Journal of Speech-Language Pathology, 14,* 172–186.

Fisher, W., Piazza, C. C., Bowman, L. G., Hagopian, L. P., Owens, J. C., & Slevin, I. (1992). A comparison of two approaches for identifying reinforcers for persons with severe and profound disabilities. *Journal of Applied Behavior Analysis, 25,* 491–498.

Frost, L. A., & Bondy, A. S. (2002). *The Picture Exchange Communication System training manual* (2nd ed.). Newark, DE: Pyramid Educational Consultants.

Ganz, J. B., Kaylor, M., Bourgeois, B., & Hadden, K. (2008). The impact of social scripts and visual cues on verbal communication in three children with autism spectrum disorders. *Focus on Autism and Other Developmental Disabilities, 23,* 79–94.

Ganz, J. B., & Simpson, R. L. (2004). Effects on communicative requesting and speech development of the Picture Exchange Communication System in children with characteristics of autism. *Journal of Autism and Developmental Disorders, 34,* 395–409.

Gasalberti, D. (2006). Alternative therapies for children and youth with special health care needs. *Journal of Pediatric Health Care, 20,* 133–136.

Goldstein, H. (2002). Communication intervention for children with autism: A review of treatment efficacy. *Journal of Autism and Developmental Disorders, 32,* 373–396.

Goldstein, H., Kaczmarek, L., Pennington, R., & Shafer, K. (1992). Peer-mediated intervention: Attending to, commenting on, and acknowledging the behavior of preschoolers with autism. *Journal of Applied Behavior Analysis, 25,* 289–305.

Granpeesheh, D., Tarbox, J., Dixon, D. R., Wilke, A. E., Allen, M. S., & Bradstreet, J. J. (2009). Randomized trial of hyperbaric oxygen therapy for children with autism. *Research in Autism Spectrum Disorders, 4,* 268–275.

Gray, C. (2002). *The sixth sense II*. Arlington, TX: Future Horizons.

Gray, C. (2010). *The new social story book* (10th ed.). Arlington, TX: Future Horizons.

Iwata, B. A., Dorsey, M. F., Slifer, K. J., Bauman, K. E., & Richman, G. S. (1994). Toward a functional analysis of self-injury. *Journal of Applied Behavior Analysis, 27,* 197–209.

Jahr, E. (2001). Teaching children with autism to answer novel wh-questions by utilizing a multiple exemplar strategy. *Research in Developmental Disabilities, 22,* 407–423.

Kahng, S., Iwata, B. A., DeLeon, I. G., & Worsdell, A. S. (1997). Evaluation of the "control over reinforcement" component in functional communication training. *Journal of Applied Behavior Analysis, 30,* 267–277.

Kamps, D. M., Leonard, B. R., Vernon, S., Dugan, E. P., & Delquadri, J. C. (1992). Teaching social skills to students with autism to increase peer interactions in an integrated first-grade classroom. *Journal of Applied Behavior Analysis, 25,* 281–288.

Koegel, L. K. (1995). Communication and language intervention. In R. L. Koegel & L. K. Koegel (Eds.), *Teaching children with autism: Strategies for initiating positive interactions and improving learning opportunities* (pp. 17–32). Baltimore, MD: Brookes.

Koegel, L. K. (2000). Interventions to facilitate communication in autism. *Journal of Autism and Developmental Disorders, 30,* 383–391.

Koegel, L. K., Koegel, R. L., Frea, W. D., & Fredeen, R. M. (2001). Identifying early intervention targets for children with autism in inclusive school settings. *Behavior Modification, 25,* 745–761.

Landa, R. (2000). Social language use in Asperger syndrome and high-functioning autism. In A. Klin, F. R. Volkmar, & S. S. Sparrow (Eds.), *Asperger syndrome* (pp. 125–155). New York, NY: Guilford Press.

Laushey, K. M., & Heflin, L. J. (2000). Enhancing social skills of kindergarten children with autism through the training of multiple peers as tutors. *Journal of Autism and Developmental Disorders, 30,* 183–193.

Lerman, D. C., & Vorndran, C. M. (2002). On the status of knowledge for using punishment: Implications for treating behavior disorders. *Journal of Applied Behavior Analysis, 35,* 431–464.

Lerman, D. C., Vorndran, C. M., Addison, L., & Kuhn, S. C. (2004). Preparing teachers in evidence-based practices for young children with autism. *School Psychology Review, 33,* 510–526.

Liddle, K. (2001). Implementing the picture exchange communication system (PECS). *International Journal of Language and Communication Disorders, 36,* 391–395.

Matson, J. (2009). Aggression and tantrums in children with autism: A review of behavioral treatments and maintaining variables. *Journal of Mental Health Research in Intellectual Disabilities, 2,* 169–187.

Matson, J. L., & Boisjoli, J. A. (2009). The token economy for children with intellectual disability and/or autism: A review. *Research in Developmental Disabilities, 30,* 240–248.

Mesibov, G. B. (1986). A cognitive program for teaching social behaviors to verbal autistic adolescents and adults. In E. Schopler & G. B. Mesibov (Eds.), *Social behavior in autism.* (pp. 265–283). New York, NY: Plenum Press.

Mesibov, G. B., Adams, L. W., & Klinger, L. G. (1997). *Autism: Understanding the disorder.* New York, NY: Plenum Press.

Mesibov, G. B., Shea, V., & Schopler, E. (2004). *The TEACCH approach to autism spectrum disorders.* New York, NY: Springer.

Mirenda, P. (2008). A back door approach to autism and AAC. *Augmentative and Alternative Communication, 24,* 220–234.

Noens, I. L. J., & van Berckelaer-Onnes, I. A. (2005). Captured by details: Sense-making, language and communication in autism. *Journal of Communication Disorders, 38,* 123–141.

Northup, J., Wacker, D., Sasso, G., Steege, M., Cigrand, K., Cook, J., & DeRaad, A. (1991). A brief functional analysis of aggressive and alternative behavior in an outclinic setting. *Journal of Applied Behavior Analysis, 24,* 509–522.

Odom, S. L., Brown W. H., Frey, T., Karasu, N., Smith-Canter, L. L., & Strain, P. S. (2003). Evidence-based practices for young children with autism: Contributions for single-subject design research. *Focus on Autism and Other Developmental Disabilities, 18,* 166–175.

Pennington, B. F. (2002). *The development of psychopathology: Nature and nurture.* New York, NY: Guilford Press.

Roane, H. S., Vollmer, T. R., Ringdahl, J. E., & Marcus, B. A. (1998). Evaluation of a brief stimulus preference assessment. *Journal of Applied Behavior Analysis, 31,* 605–620.

Rogers, S. J. (2000). Interventions that facilitate socialization in children with autism. *Journal of Autism and Developmental Disorders, 30,* 399–413.

Rose, R., & Anketell, C. (2009). The benefits of social skills groups for young people with autism spectrum disorder: A pilot study. *Child Care in Practice, 15,* 127–144.

Ruble, L., Willis, H., & Crabtree, V. M. (2008). Social skills group therapy for autism spectrum disorders. *Clinical Case Studies, 7,* 287–300.

Saunders, R. R., McEntee, J. E., & Saunders, M. D. (2005). Interaction of reinforcement schedules, a behavioral prosthesis, and work-related behavior in adults with mental retardation. *Journal of Applied Behavior Analysis, 38,* 163–176.

Schepis, M. M., Reid, D. H., Fitzgerald, J. R., Faw, G. D., van den Pol, R. A., & Welty, P. A. (1982). A program for increasing manual signing by autistic and profoundly retarded youth within the daily environment. *Journal of Applied Behavior Analysis, 15,* 363–379.

Skokut, M., Robinson, S., Openden, D., & Jimerson, S. R. (2008). Promoting the social and cognitive competence of children with autism: Interventions at school. *The California School Psychologist, 13,* 93–107.

Spencer, T. D., Peterson, D. B., & Gillam, S. L. (2008). Picture exchange communication system (PECS) or sign language: An evidence-based decision-making example. *Teaching Exceptional Children, 41,* 40–47.

Steege, M. W., Wacker, D. P., Cigrand, K. C., Berg, W. K., Novak, C. G., Reimers, T. M., . . . & DeRaad, A. (1990). Use of negative reinforcement in the treatment of self-injurious behavior. *Journal of Applied Behavior Analysis, 23,* 459–467.

Stokes, T. (1992). Discrimination and generalization. *Journal of Applied Behavior Analysis, 25,* 429–432.

Stokes, T. F., & Baer, D. M. (1977). An implicit technology of generalization. *Journal of Applied Behavior Analysis, 10,* 349–367.

Tincani, M. (2004). Comparing the picture exchange communications system and sign language training for children with autism. *Focus on Autism and Other Developmental Disabilities, 19,* 152–163.

Volden, J., & Lord, C. (1991). Neologisms and idiosyncratic language in autistic speakers. *Journal of Autism and Developmental Disorders, 21,* 109–130.

Volden, J., Mulcahy, R. F., & Holdgrafer, G. (1997). Pragmatic language disorder and perspective taking in autistic speakers. *Applied Psycholinguistics, 18,* 181–198.

Volkmar, F. R., & Lord, C. (2007). Diagnosis and definition of autism and other pervasive developmental disorders. In F. R. Volkmar (Ed.), *Autism and pervasive developmental disorders* (2nd ed.; pp. 1–31). New York, NY: Cambridge University Press.

Vollmer, T. R. (2002). Punishment happens: Some comments on Lerman and Vorndran's review. *Journal of Applied Behavior Analysis, 35,* 469–473.

Vollmer, T. R., & Iwata, B. A. (1991). Establishing operations and reinforcement effects. *Journal of Applied Behavior Analysis, 24,* 279–291.

Vollmer, T. R., Iwata, B. A, Zarcone, J. R., Smith, R. G., & Mazaleski, J. (1993). The role of attention in the treatment of attention-maintained self-injurious behavior:

Noncontingent reinforcement and differential reinforcement of other behavior. *Journal of Applied Behavior Analysis, 26,* 9–21.

Vollmer, T. R., Marcus, B., & Ringdahl, J. (1995). Noncontingent escape as treatment for self-injurious behavior maintained by negative reinforcement. *Journal of Applied Behavior Analysis, 28,* 15–26.

Woods, T. S. (1982). Reducing severe aggressive and self-injurious behavior: A nonintrusive, home based approach. *Behavioral Disorders, 7,* 180–188.

Yoder, P., & McDuffie, A. (2006). Teaching young children with autism to talk. *Seminars in Speech & Language, 27,* 161–172.

Yoder, P. J., Spruytenburg, H., Edwards, A., & Davies, B. (1995). Effect of verbal routine contexts and expansions on gains in the mean length of utterance in children with developmental delays. *Language, Speech, and Hearing Services in Schools, 26,* 21–32.

Tammy D. Barry, Ph.D., is a child clinical psychologist and assistant professor in the Department of Psychology at The University of Southern Mississippi (USM). She obtained her M.A. and Ph.D. from The University of Alabama and completed her clinical internship at the University of Alabama at Birmingham School of Medicine Department of Psychiatry and Behavioral Neurobiology. After the internship, Dr. Barry worked as a post-doctoral research fellow and adjunct assistant professor in the Department of Psychology at The University of Alabama. During that time, she also provided services and supervision at The University of Alabama Autism Spectrum Disorders Research Clinic. Dr. Barry served as a visiting assistant professor at The University of Louisville and an assistant professor at Texas A&M University before joining the faculty at USM. Dr. Barry's current research interests focus on child externalizing behaviors (e.g., Attention Deficit/Hyperactivity Disorder, Oppositional Defiant Disorder, Conduct Disorder, aggression), as well as autism spectrum disorders. Specifically, Dr. Barry is interested in exploring contextual and biological correlates, including moderators and mediators, of these psychological disorders in children.

Stephanie H. Bader is currently a student in the doctoral program in clinical psychology at The University of Southern Mississippi (USM). Before attending USM, Bader received her B.A. from Binghamton University, The State University of New York, in psychology with an emphasis in applied behavior analysis (ABA). Bader has assessment and intervention experience with children with ASD in school settings, outpatient clinics, and private practice settings. Her research focuses on parenting factors and associated behaviors of ASD.

Theodore S. Tomeny graduated from Spring Hill College in Mobile, AL and is currently a student in the doctoral program in clinical psychology at The University of Southern Mississippi. Tomeny has worked with children with ASD in both clinical and research settings. His current research focuses on family dynamics of children with ASD, including risk factors and outcomes of their siblings.

Printed in the United States
by Baker & Taylor Publisher Services